Excommunicated
(A Bard's Tale)

Poetry Blog: www.amazulugaming.com
Instagram: Onepoeticgamer
Twitch: www.twitch.tv/onepoeticgamer

ISBN 979-8-9857102-1-2

Published by
AmaZulu Gaming, LLC

Front cover art work done by Jarred Simmons
Back cover art work done by Christopher Roland

Final Edition
Printed in the United States of America

Table of Contents

February 3rd

19 Minutes......................................7
CICU 10 (Long Walk)......................10
Sitting With Indefinite...;;..................11
Black Whole...................................12
Mental Health.................................13
The Other Side of Parallel..................15
Poetic Flows - 2..............................16
Shadow Work..................................18
The Release....................................19
The Fall..21

15:51

Programming..................................23
After The Dissolution........................24
Out From Underground......................26
Poetic Prism...................................27
The Moment of Freedom.....................28
Public Esoteric Poetry........................29
The Other Side of Balance...................31
Unfettered......................................32
While You Busy Being Them................33
When Asked....................................34

"I Got You"

I Choose..36
Just Because....................................37
Memories Return..............................38
Similar Things.................................39
Soulful Relic...................................40
Within a Prayers Reach......................41
To Be..43
In The Meantime..............................44
In Place, In Space.............................45
No Need to Switch............................47

One of Few……………………………..……..49
Normally Ordinary………....…..……………......51
Hoping You...………………………….............53
E in Motion…………………………..………..55
Excommunicated…..……………………..………..56

When Darkness Won't Evade
There's Always A Light That Shines
To Bring About Balance Between The Two

-Poetic

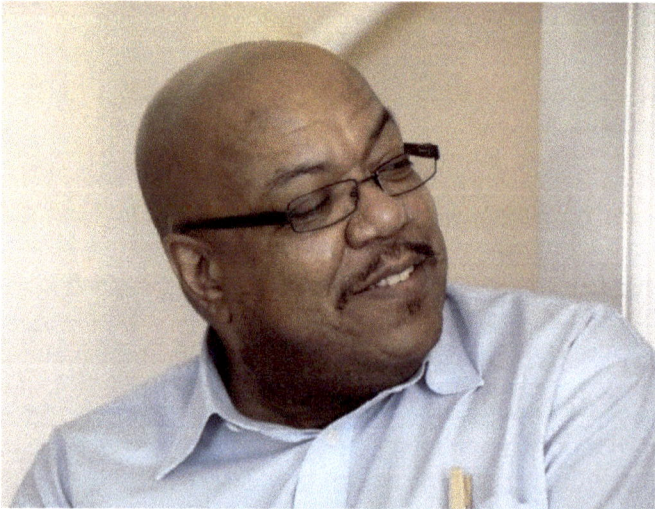

Dedication/Preface

This poetry book is dedicated to and the memory of my uncle, Ronnie T Williams. Since I have rarely expressed my feelings of his passing up to this day, these poems are my reactions and reflections from that energy. My Uncle Ronnie was a huge part of my life, the big brother I always wanted and never thought I had until he was gone. He was the one that introduced me to video games, provided me with soul music from different eras and on and on and on. He made time to listen or support me in regards to my poetry throughout all the years I have written. This book encapsulates our many conversations and while limited to a few poems (as I could never write the depths of our ventures), it does speak on the things we would express to each other and I would find some way to make it into a poem. I won't say it was hard to write this, but the amount of emotion in creating this was almost overwhelming. There were times I was penning a few of these poems and steadily crying. I cried while organizing and rewriting the book. I cried just sitting there alone thinking about memories. I'm sure I'll continue to cry about it all but not because I'm sad, but as a means of releasing. I miss my Uncle Ronnie dearly and I know that one day we will be reconnected in energy to enjoy new times and experiences. This one is for you "Unc".

February 3rd

-When Darkness Won't Evade-

19 Minutes
(Big Brother)

Find myself drifting
thinking of stuff I have to tell you
hit you on text and say call me
these thoughts are special
but then I blank to
and remember you have transitioned
nodding my head to
the beat of my heart missing
tears overflowing
mind going in so many ways
what was I doing, lost in my thoughts
stuck in this haze
days run together, time has eclipsed
back track my steps
beside bewildered
asking what am I to do next
in line for therapy, resynchronizing
my soul in cardiac arrest
no one to save me, you could embrace the
heart stopped inside my chest
and yet can feel things slipping
I'm wishing, if things were different
scenarios paid out
but wasn't paying attention
and that's a given, listening to the sound of
things falling apart
how is it that things are finished
when I don't know where to start

a part now gone forever
a lost art now arched
in skylines, I now find myself gazing
looking at the trail, stories I'll tell
the ones we left blazing
phasing in and out, asking for the big picture
will broke and now I choke, thinking I should liquor
my way into unconsciousness
where we discuss HER
His Emotions Released, my greatest feat
poetry makes it clearer
mirror dreams personified, wide eyed at 4:44 AM
speaking to myself softly
knowing tomorrow I won't see him
it was us versus them
brainstorms that don't dim
chances moving from slim to goodie
hidden in hoodie I hang on a whim
swim throughout the madness
looking for a shore where I can recover
didn't realize it until now
I was the little bro you never had
and you were my big brother
no other way to explain it
no way we can go back
one minute I'm focused
next I'm sidetracked
lacking with no pick up
game, I'm catching flack
we are wolves that stick together
souls from the same pack

won't ask no higher being
it wouldn't change any fact
if this was win or losing
I've lost, mentally clapped
am I pulling the trigger
model roles you taught
mold broken when I made this figure
I figure no time will heal
looking for room to breathe
waiting to exhale
will I ever find reprieve…

CICU 10
(Long Walk)

Don't much matter when
everything that made sense
in the past, what did hurt
has me currently embracing it
from shock to numb
what's love got to do with this
doctors giving reports and
I'm on the sideline looking translucent
playing music, to move his
soul to the flow of life's movements
man is literally living in the machine
I sit silent as tears visually mix
thoughts up in the air
it's not supposed to be like this
lost for words, light seems dark
soul searching as his mind forgets.

Sitting with Indefinite

Time has shifted
and I use to need you for your tangibles
but then the fog lifted
situated somewhere in between
two fires came the blizzard
now, daily doses aren't enough
when getting hit with mixes
that circumvent reactions
as if drugs were being injected
I'm the sheep colored black
a shadow bringer whose light is antiseptic
intercepted energy not meant for me
clairsentient that's balancing
codes the current matrix deems a threat
to firewalls that wish to reject
it's, not enough for those conditioned
freedom is but a word to these
so I sit away, appearing lonely
only to be found holding perpetuity.

Black Whole

I was told black holes exist
to suck life into a new creation
complacent in this arrangement
making this an estrangement of thought
settle to infinite within this dark light
years apart are minutes to energy
or souls cast for the unscripted movie
at first, I used indoctrinated methods for comfort
but that was released quick
when uncertainty requires creativity
that in which I was shun for
to make the best out of current situations
that need 90% of brain power
theory claims is never used
that same now that concludes
this is how the black hole moves
I wonder if I crusade in the name of it,
if apocalyptic scriptures would be written
for explanation in minds to understand
what inner self already comprehends
when finding tunes to develop intuition
do the opposite of feel
and make like this black hole
of which rules of astrophysics give in
to the gravity of perception.

Mental Health

Silent killer
the kind that, the police can't find
sitting in the back of the mind
waiting…
waiting for the day
the hour
minute
second
each breath the last
or…the first,
what's worse is it feels no one listens
feels like I should mention
a thousand love yous
are needed
for every dream where I'm defeated
thought I could beat this
support when I bleed this
pain…
the mind is a terrible thing to waste
and yet I sit in this mental wasteland
waiting to be released
from demons I didn't ask for
nor know how to conquer
why bother
if I feel there is no longer a reason to live
please believe

I'm looking amiss the fog
amongst this pressure of peers
waiting,
for that day I can identify
sunshine.

The Other Side of Parallel

I search for the courage to kill myself
to phase out of my illusions
won't waste time on therapeutic solutions
my choice is above suggestion
and anyone's judgement
debating the finite mind
with thoughts that aren't mine
while leveling between
my bio suit and energy
moving in non-descriptive motions
much like a maybe that may be
the reason I no longer look for
in retrospective
and my perspective
questions how much real I have consumed
during this journey,
got enough wait for it
to make it to yesterday
and while the universe experiences itself
I experience the universe at my expense
here's to a wish upon a star that's fallen
yet still twinkles in the eye
and I, I…
search for the courage to will myself
as a phase in on this side
of life.

Poetic Flows - 2

I live on the edge of society
a place many won't go to
because to do so
would mean you'd join an outcast
without a mask
you'd have to want to be here
whether it's to comfort my need
or, unconditional love has you planting seeds
either way, there must be fulfillment
from drinking cups half empty
grateful for just an opportunity
there's nothing new to my soul
only me, this being,
human
is what sets me up for this lesson
this education of sorts
where I can remember past lifetimes
but I grind to find a means to ascend
from greatness, my fate is
predestined in soul contracts
predicated by free will
so if you will, indulge me with
your experiences and stories
maybe I'll catch a whiff
and get a better understanding
while you standing over me
suppose to be harmony on the thin line
where I signed up for this
called to duty to find peace on interstellar dreams

so while I trek the stars, wars are conscripted
by others that lack healing
feels like I'm stealing from one hand
just to give to the other
then shrug my shoulders when asked
why I reflect through projections
nudge self and say I'm just messin' with ya
bad joke, let me stand up
take this mic stand and spit poetry
through amplifiers so my vibes
cause sound waves to make sense in your ear
and what got me here, to this place
the edge of society
was me looking for sobriety
from running out somehow
on this timeline.

Shadow Work

Take good vibes only
and rid me of this nonsense
I don't repent on what help make me
shadows found daily
by those seeking light
I am the night, the other side to your vibe
inside this luminous darkness
I find balance
not perceived karma, my life's work
is equal to it its worth in ancient timelines
and present day
cast stones if you will
and ill won't require the use of masks
vaccines or chemical complexes
perspective is as fitting as
the person reading this lyric,
rejecting souls in dualities of end time destinations
you're walking either in heaven or hell
and if conscious enough
your sub, cons us into thinking
that participating without the heat
is logical,
where you stand can make you diabolical
love long enough and hate will make you a villain,
who's winning if somebody must lose
despite what I choose
I sit with the dark side of the force
holding light,
because shadows can only be made when
something or someone
shines bright.

The Release
(That feeling that I get)

When thinking of the ones
that returned back to energy
serving me through memories
attached to me spiritually
depending on your ethnicity
or how you were raised individually
has everything to do
on if and how you're feeling me
what I see is not the same visually
taught to us on third dimension
so I upgraded to 11 D
use to prefer those that had double Ds
got off those limitations
and entered inner symmetry
aligned with all the stars
so you could say she's really into me
I definitely can feel the change
healed from past history
suffered losses til I realized the victory
was me just getting up
defeat is not my destiny
unexpectedly out the blue
ascension nothing new
this how I do it presently
heads up not a requirement
I'm outer space and watching comfortably
from over there cause when I'm here
it's like witnessing an anomaly

partially, particularly
my particles are positioning
next to God or Most High
whatever suits your theology
hearsay not the same
when it comes out truthfully
so consider this my gospel
this walk on Earth is heavenly
seventy's kid but an old soul
I've been around for eternity.

The Fall
(Feel The)

I don't know if
the pain is more from the let down
that came with us falling out
or
how hard it felt when
I lowered myself from this high frequency
when I tried to coincide
with you.

15:51

There's Always A Light That
Shines

Programming

These aren't shadows
or darkness,
not negative confused with
hard times
you want in on my mind
when I'm outside of it
beside this
next to nothing
collective saying it has to be something
but there's no script
no, way of thinking I follow
can't make me a leader
a strategic planner that
makes all the wrong assumptions
gets glorified for being a forward thinker
moving ass backwards
capture the moment yet demand freedom
figuring this is polar opposites
but can't really say
where the universe ends, begins
or extends out in another form of space
debate that while I figure
using figures know as symbols
that symbolize that potential
of this verse, these words
that don't make the world turn
but turn into thoughts derailed
untrained so that my mind can grow
without going through programming
again and again and again and…

After the Dissolution

My perfect imperfection
played chase while endlessly napping
this is me reaching
the other side of the board to be crowned
checking for mate sake
you could say one thing, feel another
and determine neither spoke to soul
algorithm running rampant
besiege it with yield signs
find pacemakers outside the heart
keep that in mind,
as keeps are finding themselves lost
on one way streets while crossing sidewalks
could be I'm random
but I'd rather taste the results of honey bees
that's actually bittersweet
hanging over after one
to many means we should do this solo
then again, I don't know
if the point is as effective when dull
nullified the effects just to see how you're affected
I'm left with choices to my own devices
kind of hard to be nice when
I say I'm mean softly
no harm to pierced ear,
drums ringing the alarm
split from conditioned contradiction
here's the withdrawn band to prove it

and I never knew this ultimately lead
to the same flame twice
once upon a time
after noon left morning
to day dream.

Out from Underground

Light body holding its shadow
this perception is not equal to what was thought,
doesn't represent total truth
rooted up since directions are more so old news
love is just love
and not made for comparison
nor to be sold for gratification
as instant access leads to less appreciation
why questions not made for doctrine
infused into the masses
I read life not written in books
get called different since
my time is before acceptance
let us count sheep while sleep
pointing at those that are black
in thought while meditating
levitating in non-binary form
the jury is out despite a judge free zone
far gone yet here we are
open to interstellar limits
turning the visit to permanent
since I'm out from the protection of
the underground.

Poetic Prism

I defy language through my feelings
when writing words that spark healing
so you won't find me kneeling
looking up for something not in the ceiling
realizing the ever-verse on the inside of me
and how I was taught to distant this energy
for others that only cipher
making up what I'm supposed to be
freely give up what makes me shine eternally
just because there are those that are greedy
once needy, moving slow but speedy
upgrade to lead from BBs
then cop her from my readings
teething on my thoughts
and soul claps that seed through jism
create the status quo
from underground poetic prisms.

The Moment of Freedom

I spoke with my soul today
and cried spirit like tears
from realizing
how in past situations
I abandoned self
looked for help through the experience
of someone else
and kept listening to everyone
except me,
not hating on what was done
or
unforgiving to choices made
this was the moment that's been in the making
for eons
waiting for the process
trusting the inside
while sitting outside of the desires
of any others' control,
today I turned
stopped running and,
enjoyed the harmony I've sought
since time was birthed
from creation.

.

Public Esoteric Poetry

I need you to innerstand
cause outside of these walls
is a tall tale that a collective
makes for you to believe
Geez, us vs cream puff marshmallow men
is the same as accepting "them"
like a color
can't think of no other way to say it
convey these lines and find
myself alone with everybody
or should I say a lot of bodies
that's selling, the truth I'm telling
has me building up free time
on unlimited data plans labeled Infiniti
meanwhile, somewhere in Japan
I'm driven to write lyrics with luxury status
of Universal Mathematics
now we can speak, even though I know
you don't get it…but do
just because - she's personified victory
placed under-Neith I seek things
a little differently
meditating in day dreams and speak to
self, cause moves up-bringing
didn't necessarily teach me correctly
professed self to unlearn just to remember
you want to know where I'm going

meet me in the grocery store
so I can feed you knowledge
with or without college
it's your choice what to eat
choose wisely…

The Other Side of Balance

If my steps away from the collective
bothers you
then choice bounds me
to embrace love between our disagreement
or
make arrangements to vacate my stay,
either way a fight of sorts is at play
one without the need of fists
which, is just as enduring
when one is aware at several levels.

Unfettered

Vibes on tilt
at a cosmic level
cast at all pivots
found at the opposites
of known elements
refreshed negative ions
inhaled from rain
smack laced with dope
taken straight to my brain
and, love went beyond feels
unconditional with intent
as someday it will come
despite already being here
choosing instead of wanting
unsaid yet accepted.

While You Busy Being Them

Instead of backwards manifesting
I relearned so many lessons
let go of all the stressing
air head that's somehow breathless
went from literal to less -ing
all the illusions now undressing
confessing not a ritual
balanced overused aggression
society no longer messing
no pressure to feel less then
racing with other humans
but not blinded by their conceptions
stop measuring my success with
checks for equal blessings
we shinning whenever needed
in shadows, that's where I rest-in
take chances and believe it
what I do, fulfills a need
many aspire to be a rose
I'm satisfied being a weed.

When Asked

I'm nothing of what they say I should be
and that's exactly how it will remain
so let's share love
a collective of things that's always been
because that's when it's true
and why won't matter
since where this is coming from
makes me everything
of what I am.

"I Got You"

To Bring About Balance
Between The Two

I Choose

When asked
why try the impossible
I felt the thought over with intuition
and, decided it's better for me to choose
then wait to be chosen
no matter the outcome waiting
on the other side.

Just Because

Snapped out of a deep sleep
a moment of recognition
I need not the words to explain the meaning
and I've been meaning to give you this,
this unfiltered version of love
not subjected to standards
spinning on parallel times
where I shorten the distance
from the "longing urge"
to "thoughts that merge"
present choice into byproducts of unity
wasn't sure at first what to call it
then, when
presented with the taste of pure
it was there we sat within to relish
unlocked forgotten pleasantries
a need recognized
and here, you and I can finally converse
mix in with each other so our skin blends
amend ancient karma
so the transit then transfers
from dueling to dual lovers
that lay in the comforts of
memories we create
face to face
heart to heart
soul to soul
let me say it, I love you
just because.

Memories Return

Port cleared to allow
loads that move up and down
and now, I recollect the bits and pieces
to make sense of the unconscious
with death causing emptiness
there are vacancies ready to be filled
move these unemployed feelings
that now work as if it's play
days unnamed let loose of time
where I'm found listening to silence
hearing intuition, thinking about blue pills
that leave many in ignorant bliss
the taste of sweet contradiction
a welcomed poisonous elixir
I've detoxed from the fix,
armed with the force yet not forcing choice
choosing overcast since it mixes shades
it's a way to appreciate the grays
that lay somewhere off the grid
amongst stars aimed at
but not reached for reasons
I'm standing under
and I no longer protest against these memories
upon their return.

Similar Things

Over time
we chose to
inosculate our souls
for all to see
but not many know,
conversing with
the use of silence
a love unconditional
light being intimate
with darkness
signatures written
on air
into skies that
show us a picture
of others
that reminiscence on
similar things.

Soulful Relic

Be my original truth
symbols that will symbol
the heart of who you are,
buried artifact that in fact
is sought out by millions
a keystone I've come home to remember
a secret kept secret in plain view
outlined by features of your soul
unexposed and yet, outright expression
I heard you from light years away
couldn't help but come to you
as you're all that matters
or at least that's what I choose.

Within a Prayers Reach
(for HER)

This is the savoring of words
that lift from my pallet
allocated by the number of syllables
so each could maturate into the habit
of knowing you - holding you
by means of acoustic fervor
treasure the peace in the release of the beat,
is this comfortable enough for your pleasure
whether or not, let this assure your belief
boxed in the search for love
which lead me to your light
bright illuminations found without sight
write words to instruments then silently recite
loose with, what's translucent
above, you descend
it's a movement that flies with a dove
so let's do this, I ascend
joined as one, we make love
and now lucent
what we are, they think of
and you have to be the tear that
appears from my eye
when I lay back and experience the universe
conversely, I may be feeling the afterthought
to prayers ancestors sent for an angel that went
the extra mile and lent patience until we met
and felt in free will
so we could wield this exact moment

cause don't it - seem like - a movie
watching us on screen and you're beside me
popping corn in your mouth and déjà vu is about
to have us experience the glitch in the matrix
look at each other and feel this
was what was meant in the freedom
fought to give this opportunity today
where we choose each other
so within, is without...asé.

To Be

She cried stars and crystals
by which particles existed
so our mix while quantum
is felt by the masses
in all directions
pure love unconditional
that's chosen to occur
in this frame of time
from her tears that dry up
forming stardust that fertilizes
life, my life
a most beautiful creation
exemplified by the process of be.

In The Meantime
(The Wait for You)

How it feels
isn't really how it is
despite the soul connection
why did we choose to live like this
can see you sending messages
on things we can relate
but here I'm laying lonely
pillow looking me in the face
hate to use hate to feel better
wishing love would take its place
meanwhile watching social media
eye illusions got my mind laced
heart needs to keep beating
thoughts say this time we waste
make moves to get much closer
moving at a snails pace
tasting the victory
in every defeat that comes with haste
wait - this is it, there's the proof
will he survive, seeking the truth
this is it, here's the proof
is death an opening
is living just uncouth?

In Place, In Space

Let's move past nature laws
mix physical and intangible
then find us in the mix
switch from dreamlike voids
to lucid realities
lost in bizarre
only to find normalcy is our difference
guiding us across twisted paths
that lead to moving straight backwards
ain't that peculiar
Earth timelines vortex in a place called space
behind so we meet somewhere in the middle
fiddle with the thought of
paying off karma
then cashing in on opportunities
sift through the clutter of love
to cuddle you in the midst of chaos
you could then say I found peace
in the way that breathes
but left me breathless
if this is helplessness
then my inn-er dependence
lives outside your walls
looking at you peep through a hole
so while watching me
this tunnel vision has laser focus
and leaves me sleeping on you
or on the side
then have the nerve to stay woke

just to see how beautiful you are
in addition to your regular
however, shake my hand with the use of the other
that way we're still holding one another
without contempt
seal our approval for love down payments
peculiar, ain't it
in a space on this place called
Earth.

No Need to Switch

Face the facts of the matter
some may not be feelings this
didn't know it would happen
that I'm in love with a witch
you busy casting judgement
since society says they're different
won't beg to differ
just for you to take notice
hold those preconceived beliefs
while we wear freedom coated
in truths religions practice
shrug shoulders for those
thinking I might be enchanted
yet in reversal, I cast spells poetically
can find evidence in my lyrics
within the embodiment
moon tattoos in crescent
visual quite pleasant
it's too late to save the republic
but maybe this woman can
again, universal magic happens
no matter if you think it exist
crafts she enact are strange
but that's to the uninitiated
so while you fear what you don't understand
I'm busy giving her a spiritual kiss
to her face and the fact of the matter
is some may not be feelings this
but why waste my life on what you want

that gives me no reason to switch
so I focus, not hocus pocus
manifest energy rooted deep
through plants she shares love with
so is this, will it, benefit the bliss
hooded in balance
grey skies are the perfect mix
wrapped up in beaded bracelets around my wrist
why waste a wish when what I dream
is right here in existence
and, let's face the fact of this matter
there won't be no need to switch
nature in her element
and he is the alchemist.

One of Few

She vampires my thoughts
so I rely on intuition to save me
or maybe, this thinking is worth the sacrifice
when looking for me at night
she'll find a lone wolf howling at reflected light
alchemized moonshine that we'll delight
in taste, mix match our intensity
efficiently til kundalini awakes
scripted way before our time here
it appears I'm drawn to you
stenciling in a word envisioned by the mind's eye
U-N-I...T-Y
involve you and I speaking languages
coded in secrecy for everybody to hear
the sheer thought of love equating math
or a whole made up of half
two odd pieces intact and I'm left to ask
is this even right
it's like, on one end
I desire a human need for communication
as I perceive you through senses
that don't require touch
feel me up with such emotions
I'd follow you without pushing a butt-on
could we be on to somethin'
or is this just another play on words
confused with magic, defying logic
and as I await your response
I embellish in voice notes not left for me

but I make believe until the dream is true
until soft lips sing to me
from a source deep within the surface
of a flat earth,
imperfect mold that's beautiful
that many say is taboo
I guess, I'm one of the few.

Normally Ordinary

Many wanted Marilyn
I only needed Norma Jean
set in jeans being normal
let her genes do what's natural
attract me,
she had me at that smile
which mirrored what I felt on the inside
decided that, on the eve of the day
before everything changed
I would mention her name
feeling the same way
for modern day goddesses
that float on my digitized magazine screen
processed queens
that truly are, except
I face their alter ego
this is no low blow
I don't know you, despite how I show who
I am from soul scriptures
do you really see the big picture
figure if we gonna involve our egos
I'll expose my weaknesses
so you can step out the ring with arms raised
belt on shoulder and the applaud of the crowd
ringing in our ears
not your finger, we past common law
and I saw this opportunity to let you know
there is submission in bending a knee
much the same as when tying shoe strings

which brings me to my point
and, many wanted Monroe
for what their eyes believed
but nobody…almost nobody
beloved Norma.

Hoping You

Been holding on to this
didn't want to believe what
my eyes were telling me
looked away when I declined to be
a part of your fan base
my love is free and unconditional
-not only-
here, hold this picture
listen to what it's telling you
because I can't make it any clearer
stood up to fear
and now I'm ready for what
I didn't even know I was asking for
it's 11:15 again and
I know you feel this synchronized moment
that won't let go of me
chaos coordinated has control of the
thoughts that I'm thinking
gotta feel my way through this
the appearance of heat waves
means the sun is out
and its flower has me
on the other side of something classical
something magical
orange colors give off this fuzzy feeling
and now I'm tempted to
catch up with that position proclamation
made in suspended time facing
if you're a pusher, I'll take a gram of that instantly

can I, will you
later on, if you're free
since I don't fit, we can create gently
feelings feeling delicious
paradoxes of logic being spiritual
I want to give to you
opposite elements that hit a sweet spot
in our soul space
talk life into dead languages
Latin-a-part the chemistry
fly away before we start
here's my heart
in 46 pieces divided by 2
this is me thinking of you
on the spectrum but
somewhere in the middle of a green hue
and maybe you can replace
the blank space that's resident
give it that energy it's due
and, I'm hoping you think
of me too.

E in Motion

No need for the undigested
or feelings buried by cultural expectations,
I need that emotion
that energy in motion
releasing thoughts powered by redemption
no means to place judgement
vast in this sea of conscription
listening in, too deep for most
possibly I'm embracing purpose
others find preposterous
am I obnoxious to consider
a parallel environment in which
positive thinking beats out anxiety
smooth out a harsh reality
then label it poetic codex
this is next to nothing
and everything at once
maybe even infinity
and there's no need for the undigested
although I hold this imperfection
of energy in motion called
emotion.

Excommunicated

Wait, hold up
someone said I had to switch
wife left in the summer time
so I tried to find my chick on Twitch
shit, couldn't get, back into it
slept in one room for months
while sitting in deaths grip
the game got out of place
so my hop got replaced like a hip
green lights became my therapy
cause I don't trust no therapist
flashing lights by men in black
but what happens when I don't forget
psycho wit, polo loco sips
might not want to hang with me
9 meters listening to milli
-ons, flown through custom grips
house party consist of one
iTunes on blast to wake the neighbors with
dark times, love flows, 2020 it's-
like voices saying Finish Him
kombat a game, fade to black
lights getting dim
because I just blew a circuit
I shoot my shot just to watch it
roll about the rim
sim my life like a video game
roll the credits at the end of the film
but when everyone left the premiere

it's just me cleaning up the gym
hoping on a bank shot
throw my life away for a buck
Milwaukee's best fills the glass
I might just end up stuck
life sucked up out of me
flattened, monster trucked
fuck, the verb type
and it's really looking grim
time moving barefoot while running out
in last place, nowhere close to them
choir boys, we were singing hymns
god like, we're like Her and Him
swim when they thought I couldn't
despite the chances looking slim
watched my uncle descend into the ground
may be I should jump in on a whim
skimmed, coach getting coached
back of the plane like this was 1950
bust my ass til the police come
defined, that's getting poached, get me
roach amongst the roaches
yet they act like he's so different
I guess life isn't supposed to be easy
my life, hell bent or heaven sent
went to the Universe
feels like it's taking forever to make a dent
sense that isn't common, it's been 40 days
check my pocket for lent, here's a hint
gentleman, that's not a gent
-trification, stay home vacations

religion stop working in elementary
I just woke up, an abomination ever since
my thoughts equate to 2 cents
sense with vision not meant to be seen
had to circumvent
vent my frustrations, who's relating
alone lying in bed
if she keep saying what she saying
something gonna end up red
with the use of lead
from pen to pad, lead from the head
so if this kills the verse and I curse
will I end up dead
I'm lead to even lesser
and asked to give more
nor'easter moving until April
May find me rolling stone doors
or…

About The Author

Billy Williams, Jr. was born to write poetry.
Poetically knows as B-Dot and OnePoeticGamer,
the life as a poet all started because of a girl back in
7th grade. Seeing he had a gift with words, he began
to use his energy to produce poetry that spoke to
various genres.

Hailing from Raleigh, North Carolina, Billy is a
poet, educator, coach, gamer, streamer and
motivator Excommunicated (A Bard's Tale) is
Billy's seventh book of published poetry, with more
poetry books to be released in the near future.

If you want to find out more information about Billy's upcoming books, you can contact him by way of e-mail at onepoeticgamer@amazulugaming.com or sending a message to him from the following website www.amazulugaming.com. If you wish to know more about his gaming/streaming life, check him at www.twitch.tv/onepoeticgamer.

Social Media Contacts

Poetry Blog: www.amazulugaming.com
Instagram: Onepoeticgamer
Twitch: www.twitch.tv/onepoeticgamer

AmaZulu Gaming, LLC

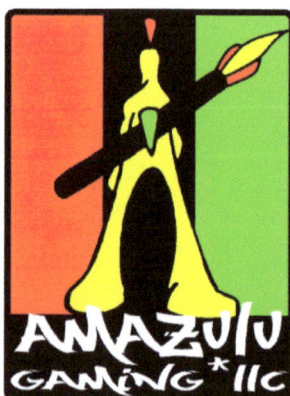

Poetry Books Written By One Poetic

Poetic Superhero

Everybody is looking for a hero. Poetic Superhero is here for you.

The I prElude I

In order to find we, HE must find himself before finding SHE.

His Emotions Released

This is written for Her…I'm glad I finally got Her attention.

School Dad

Poetry inspired by 16 years of working as an educator in elementary, middle and high school.

the Book of HER

33 poems for HER.

The Poetic Verse - My Book of Rhymes

When I feel the flow, I let go with words.

Excommunicated (A Bard's Tale)

Exit wounds given by another can lead to one's salvation.

A Bit More Than a Muse (11/11/22)

When she's a bit more than friend but doesn't recognize it yet.

HER - The Collection (Poetry Anthology) (Future Release)

Includes works from The I pr.E.lude I, His Emotions Released and the Book of HER.

<u>Spoken Word By One Poetic</u>

Poetic Acoustics (upcoming soon)

www.ingramcontent.com/pod-product-compliance
Lightning Source LLC
LaVergne TN
LVHW010310070426
835511LV00021B/3460